Wet Bandit

by Olivia White
illustrated by Sam Maldonado

Decodable 22

I0806542

Bothell, WA • Chicago, IL • Columbus, OH • New York, NY

MHEonline.com

Send all inquiries to:
McGraw-Hill Education
8787 Orion Place
Columbus, OH 43240

ISBN: 978-0-02-145445-7
MHID: 0-02-145445-0

Printed in the United States of America.

6 7 8 9 LCR 26 25 24 23

Bandit the dog got wet!
He ran in the den.

Can Jan get him?
Bandit left some hints.

Jan spots some drops.

Jan spots some big, wet prints.

But Bandit hid and hid.
He was sad.

Jan had Bandit!

Damp Bandit was glad.